THIS PRIORITY PLANNER BELONGS TO:

____

Update me on your progress
Eric@EricPapp.com

For more information on the speaking and training programs that go with this planner, please visit www.EricPapp.com

CONTENTS

HAPPINESS COMES FROM SEEING PROGRESS
IN WHAT MATTERS MOST TO YOU.

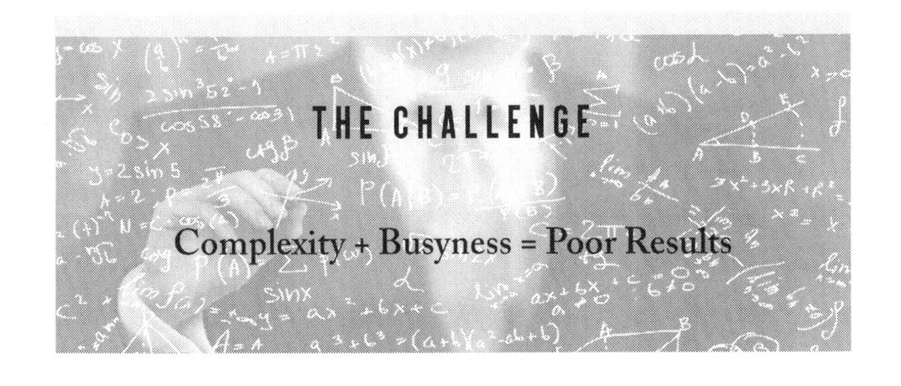

Doing More vs. Better Thinking

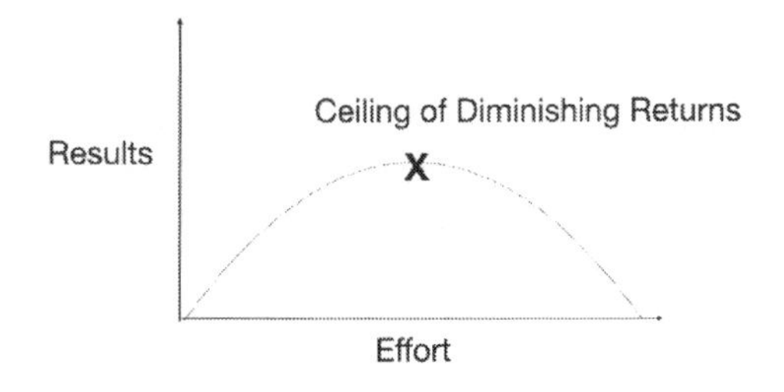

THE FALLACY OF "DOING"

- *The more I do, the more I'm worth*
- *I feel guilty when I'm not doing something*
- *I hope it's worth it in the end*

ACTIVITY DRIVES OUT THOUGHT.

THE PROBLEM

We are conditioned to believe that causes and results are equal.

Three False Beliefs:
1. Time equals value
2. Productivity equals hours worked
3. Everything is important

Mindset Shift

Switching from hours worked and effort to Impact and Results.

Swapping an 8hr workday to 3 Priorities a day.

THOSE WHO MAKE THE WORST USE OF TIME COMPLAIN OF ITS SHORTNESS.

JEAN DE LA BRUYERE

THE ANSWER

Track Progress, Prioritize, and Plan

3 Wins From Yesterday: Track Progress

- Builds your confidence and peace of mind
- Provides internal motivation
- Prevents you from measuring yourself against the ideal

3 Priorities For Today: Prioritize and Plan

- Identifies what's most important
- Overcome procrastination and perfectionism
- Time blocking provides realistic expectations

MOVE THREE PROJECTS A MILE RATHER THAN 100 "TO-DO'S" AN INCH.

YOU DON'T CONTROL YOUR ENTIRE DAY, STOP CREATING UNREALISTIC EXPECTATIONS FOR YOURSELF.

DATE : ___ / ___ / _____

3 WINS FROM YESTERDAY

1. completed project
2. made a sale
3. dinner with the family

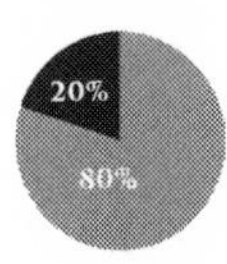

3 PRIORITIES FOR TODAY

PRIORITY #1

Outcome Finalize Presentation — Time 35min

Action Update Powerpoint and feedback from the manager — Achieved ✓

PRIORITY #2

Outcome Finish Proposal — Time 40min

Action Review other proposals and talk with John — Achieved ✓

PRIORITY #3

Outcome Book Travel — Time 60min

Action Book airfare and hotel — Achieved ✓

All three of your priorities should add up to no more than four hours.

Progress

not

Perfection

Date : ___ / ___ / _____

3 Wins From Yesterday

1. ______________________________

2. ______________________________

3. ______________________________

3 PRIORITIES FOR TODAY

20%
80%

Priority #1

Outcome ______________________ Time

Action ________________________ Achieved

Priority #2

Outcome ______________________ Time

Action ________________________ Achieved

Priority #3

Outcome ______________________ Time

Action ________________________ Achieved

____

____

QUESTIONS / NOTES

Stay Curious. Stay Creative.

DATE : ___ / ___ / _____

3 WINS FROM YESTERDAY

1. ______________________________

2. ______________________________

3. ______________________________

3 PRIORITIES FOR TODAY

PRIORITY #1

Outcome ______________________ Time

Action ______________________ Achieved

PRIORITY #2

Outcome ______________________ Time

Action ______________________ Achieved

PRIORITY #3

Outcome ______________________ Time

Action ______________________ Achieved

QUESTIONS / NOTES

Stay Curious. Stay Creative.

DATE : ___ / ___ / _____

3 WINS FROM YESTERDAY

1. ______________________________

2. ______________________________

3. ______________________________

20%
80%

3 PRIORITIES FOR TODAY

PRIORITY #1

Outcome ______________________ Time

Action ______________________ Achieved

PRIORITY #2

Outcome ______________________ Time

Action ______________________ Achieved

PRIORITY #3

Outcome ______________________ Time

Action ______________________ Achieved

____

____

QUESTIONS / NOTES

Stay Curious. Stay Creative.

DATE : ___ / ___ / _____

3 WINS FROM YESTERDAY

1. ______________________________

2. ______________________________

3. ______________________________

20%
80%

3 PRIORITIES FOR TODAY

PRIORITY #1

Outcome ______________________ Time

Action ______________________ Achieved

PRIORITY #2

Outcome ______________________ Time

Action ______________________ Achieved

PRIORITY #3

Outcome ______________________ Time

Action ______________________ Achieved

QUESTIONS / NOTES

Stay Curious. Stay Creative.

DATE : ___ / ___ / _____

3 WINS FROM YESTERDAY

1. ______________________________

2. ______________________________

3. ______________________________

20%

80%

3 PRIORITIES FOR TODAY

PRIORITY #1

Outcome ______________________ Time

Action ______________________ Achieved

PRIORITY #2

Outcome ______________________ Time

Action ______________________ Achieved

PRIORITY #3

Outcome ______________________ Time

Action ______________________ Achieved

QUESTIONS / NOTES

Stay Curious. Stay Creative.

Better Thinking Vs. More Effort

How do you work?

DATE : ___ / ___ / _____

3 WINS FROM YESTERDAY

1. ______________________________

2. ______________________________

3. ______________________________

3 PRIORITIES FOR TODAY

20%
80%

PRIORITY #1

Outcome ______________________ Time

Action ______________________ Achieved

PRIORITY #2

Outcome ______________________ Time

Action ______________________ Achieved

PRIORITY #3

Outcome ______________________ Time

Action ______________________ Achieved

____

____

QUESTIONS / NOTES

Stay Curious. Stay Creative.

DATE : ___ / ___ / _____

3 WINS FROM YESTERDAY

1. ______________________________

2. ______________________________

3. ______________________________

20%
80%

3 PRIORITIES FOR TODAY

PRIORITY #1

Outcome ______________________ Time

Action ______________________ Achieved

PRIORITY #2

Outcome ______________________ Time

Action ______________________ Achieved

PRIORITY #3

Outcome ______________________ Time

Action ______________________ Achieved

____

____

QUESTIONS / NOTES

Stay Curious. Stay Creative.

DATE : ___ / ___ / _____

3 WINS FROM YESTERDAY

1. ______________________________

2. ______________________________

3. ______________________________

20%
80%

3 PRIORITIES FOR TODAY

PRIORITY #1

Outcome ______________________ Time

Action ______________________ Achieved

PRIORITY #2

Outcome ______________________ Time

Action ______________________ Achieved

PRIORITY #3

Outcome ______________________ Time

Action ______________________ Achieved

____

____

QUESTIONS / NOTES

Stay Curious. Stay Creative.

DATE : ___ / ___ / _____

3 WINS FROM YESTERDAY

1. ______________________________

2. ______________________________

3. ______________________________

20%
80%

3 PRIORITIES FOR TODAY

PRIORITY #1

Outcome ______________________ Time

Action ______________________ Achieved

PRIORITY #2

Outcome ______________________ Time

Action ______________________ Achieved

PRIORITY #3

Outcome ______________________ Time

Action ______________________ Achieved

QUESTIONS / NOTES

Stay Curious. Stay Creative.

DATE : ___ / ___ / _____

3 WINS FROM YESTERDAY

1. ______________________________

2. ______________________________

3. ______________________________

20%
80%

3 PRIORITIES FOR TODAY

PRIORITY #1

Outcome ______________________ Time

Action ______________________ Achieved

PRIORITY #2

Outcome ______________________ Time

Action ______________________ Achieved

PRIORITY #3

Outcome ______________________ Time

Action ______________________ Achieved

____

____

QUESTIONS / NOTES

Stay Curious. Stay Creative.

How can you do

a better job

of planning your week?

DATE : ___ / ___ / _____

3 WINS FROM YESTERDAY

1. ______________________________

2. ______________________________

3. ______________________________

20% 80%

3 PRIORITIES FOR TODAY

PRIORITY #1

Outcome ______________________ Time

Action ______________________ Achieved

PRIORITY #2

Outcome ______________________ Time

Action ______________________ Achieved

PRIORITY #3

Outcome ______________________ Time

Action ______________________ Achieved

____

____

QUESTIONS / NOTES

Stay Curious. Stay Creative.

DATE : ___ / ___ / _____

3 WINS FROM YESTERDAY

1. ______________________________

2. ______________________________

3. ______________________________

3 PRIORITIES FOR TODAY

20%
80%

PRIORITY #1

Outcome ______________________ Time

Action ______________________ Achieved

PRIORITY #2

Outcome ______________________ Time

Action ______________________ Achieved

PRIORITY #3

Outcome ______________________ Time

Action ______________________ Achieved

____

____

QUESTIONS / NOTES

Stay Curious. Stay Creative.

Date : ___ / ___ / _____

3 Wins From Yesterday

1. ______________________________

2. ______________________________

3. ______________________________

3 PRIORITIES FOR TODAY

20%
80%

Priority #1

Outcome ______________________ Time

Action ______________________ Achieved

Priority #2

Outcome ______________________ Time

Action ______________________ Achieved

Priority #3

Outcome ______________________ Time

Action ______________________ Achieved

____

____

QUESTIONS / NOTES

Stay Curious. Stay Creative.

Date : ___ / ___ / _____

3 Wins From Yesterday

1. ______________________________

2. ______________________________

3. ______________________________

3 PRIORITIES FOR TODAY

20%
80%

Priority #1

Outcome ______________________ Time

Action ______________________ Achieved

Priority #2

Outcome ______________________ Time

Action ______________________ Achieved

Priority #3

Outcome ______________________ Time

Action ______________________ Achieved

____

____

QUESTIONS / NOTES

Stay Curious. Stay Creative.

DATE : ___ / ___ / _____

3 WINS FROM YESTERDAY

1. ________________________________

2. ________________________________

3. ________________________________

20%
80%

3 PRIORITIES FOR TODAY

PRIORITY #1

Outcome ________________________ Time

Action __________________________ Achieved

PRIORITY #2

Outcome ________________________ Time

Action __________________________ Achieved

PRIORITY #3

Outcome ________________________ Time

Action __________________________ Achieved

____

____

QUESTIONS / NOTES

Stay Curious. Stay Creative.

Productivity,

not activity (crazy busy),

yields Success.

DATE : ___ / ___ / _____

3 WINS FROM YESTERDAY

1. ______________________________

2. ______________________________

3. ______________________________

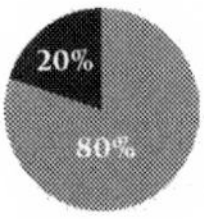

3 PRIORITIES FOR TODAY

PRIORITY #1

Outcome ______________________ Time

Action ________________________ Achieved

PRIORITY #2

Outcome ______________________ Time

Action ________________________ Achieved

PRIORITY #3

Outcome ______________________ Time

Action ________________________ Achieved

____

____

QUESTIONS / NOTES

Stay Curious. Stay Creative.

DATE : ___ / ___ / _____

3 WINS FROM YESTERDAY

1. ______________________________

2. ______________________________

3. ______________________________

3 PRIORITIES FOR TODAY

20%
80%

PRIORITY #1

Outcome ______________________ Time

Action ______________________ Achieved

PRIORITY #2

Outcome ______________________ Time

Action ______________________ Achieved

PRIORITY #3

Outcome ______________________ Time

Action ______________________ Achieved

____

____

QUESTIONS / NOTES

Stay Curious. Stay Creative.

DATE : ___ / ___ / _____

3 WINS FROM YESTERDAY

1. ______________________________

2. ______________________________

3. ______________________________

3 PRIORITIES FOR TODAY

PRIORITY #1

Outcome ______________________ Time

Action ______________________ Achieved

PRIORITY #2

Outcome ______________________ Time

Action ______________________ Achieved

PRIORITY #3

Outcome ______________________ Time

Action ______________________ Achieved

____

____

QUESTIONS / NOTES

Stay Curious. Stay Creative.

DATE : ___ / ___ / _____

3 WINS FROM YESTERDAY

1. ______________________________

2. ______________________________

3. ______________________________

3 PRIORITIES FOR TODAY

20%
80%

PRIORITY #1

Outcome ______________________ Time

Action ______________________ Achieved

PRIORITY #2

Outcome ______________________ Time

Action ______________________ Achieved

PRIORITY #3

Outcome ______________________ Time

Action ______________________ Achieved

____

____

QUESTIONS / NOTES

Stay Curious. Stay Creative.

DATE : ___ / ___ / _____

3 WINS FROM YESTERDAY

1. ________________________________

2. ________________________________

3. ________________________________

20%
80%

3 PRIORITIES FOR TODAY

PRIORITY #1

Outcome ________________________ Time

Action ________________________ Achieved

PRIORITY #2

Outcome ________________________ Time

Action ________________________ Achieved

PRIORITY #3

Outcome ________________________ Time

Action ________________________ Achieved

____

____

QUESTIONS / NOTES

Stay Curious. Stay Creative.

Take

Massive Focused

Action

DATE : ___ / ___ / _____

3 WINS FROM YESTERDAY

1. ____

2. ____

3. ____

20% 80%

3 PRIORITIES FOR TODAY

PRIORITY #1

Outcome ______________________________ Time ☐

Action ______________________________ Achieved ☐

PRIORITY #2

Outcome ______________________________ Time ☐

Action ______________________________ Achieved ☐

PRIORITY #3

Outcome ______________________________ Time ☐

Action ______________________________ Achieved ☐

____

____

QUESTIONS / NOTES

Stay Curious. Stay Creative.

DATE : ___ / ___ / _____

3 WINS FROM YESTERDAY

1. ______________________________

2. ______________________________

3. ______________________________

3 PRIORITIES FOR TODAY

20%
80%

PRIORITY #1

Outcome ______________________ Time

Action ______________________ Achieved

PRIORITY #2

Outcome ______________________ Time

Action ______________________ Achieved

PRIORITY #3

Outcome ______________________ Time

Action ______________________ Achieved

QUESTIONS / NOTES

Stay Curious. Stay Creative.

DATE : ___ / ___ / _____

3 WINS FROM YESTERDAY

1. ________________________________

2. ________________________________

3. ________________________________

20%
80%

3 PRIORITIES FOR TODAY

PRIORITY #1

Outcome ________________________ Time

Action ________________________ Achieved

PRIORITY #2

Outcome ________________________ Time

Action ________________________ Achieved

PRIORITY #3

Outcome ________________________ Time

Action ________________________ Achieved

____

____

QUESTIONS / NOTES

Stay Curious. Stay Creative.

DATE : ___ / ___ / _____

3 WINS FROM YESTERDAY

1. ________________________________

2. ________________________________

3. ________________________________

20%
80%

3 PRIORITIES FOR TODAY

PRIORITY #1

Outcome ________________________ Time

Action ________________________ Achieved

PRIORITY #2

Outcome ________________________ Time

Action ________________________ Achieved

PRIORITY #3

Outcome ________________________ Time

Action ________________________ Achieved

QUESTIONS / NOTES

Stay Curious. Stay Creative.

DATE : ___ / ___ / _____

3 WINS FROM YESTERDAY

1. ____

2. ____

3. ____

20% 80%

3 PRIORITIES FOR TODAY

PRIORITY #1

Outcome ______________________________ Time

Action ______________________________ Achieved

PRIORITY #2

Outcome ______________________________ Time

Action ______________________________ Achieved

PRIORITY #3

Outcome ______________________________ Time

Action ______________________________ Achieved

QUESTIONS / NOTES

Stay Curious. Stay Creative.

Move Three
Priorities

A Mile. Not 15

To Do's an inch.

DATE : ___ / ___ / _____

3 WINS FROM YESTERDAY

1. ______________________________

2. ______________________________

3. ______________________________

20%
80%

3 PRIORITIES FOR TODAY

PRIORITY #1

Outcome ______________________ Time

Action ______________________ Achieved

PRIORITY #2

Outcome ______________________ Time

Action ______________________ Achieved

PRIORITY #3

Outcome ______________________ Time

Action ______________________ Achieved

____

____

QUESTIONS / NOTES

Stay Curious. Stay Creative.

DATE : ___ / ___ / _____

3 WINS FROM YESTERDAY

1. ____

2. ____

3. ____

20%
80%

3 PRIORITIES FOR TODAY

PRIORITY #1

Outcome ______________________________ Time

Action ________________________________ Achieved

PRIORITY #2

Outcome ______________________________ Time

Action ________________________________ Achieved

PRIORITY #3

Outcome ______________________________ Time

Action ________________________________ Achieved

____

____

QUESTIONS / NOTES

Stay Curious. Stay Creative.

DATE : ___ / ___ / _____

3 WINS FROM YESTERDAY

1. ________________________________

2. ________________________________

3. ________________________________

20%
80%

3 PRIORITIES FOR TODAY

PRIORITY #1

Outcome ______________________ Time

Action ______________________ Achieved

PRIORITY #2

Outcome ______________________ Time

Action ______________________ Achieved

PRIORITY #3

Outcome ______________________ Time

Action ______________________ Achieved

____

____

QUESTIONS / NOTES

Stay Curious. Stay Creative.

DATE : ___ / ___ / _____

3 WINS FROM YESTERDAY

1. ______________________________

2. ______________________________

3. ______________________________

3 PRIORITIES FOR TODAY

20%

80%

PRIORITY #1

Outcome ______________________ Time

Action ______________________ Achieved

PRIORITY #2

Outcome ______________________ Time

Action ______________________ Achieved

PRIORITY #3

Outcome ______________________ Time

Action ______________________ Achieved

____

____

QUESTIONS / NOTES

Stay Curious. Stay Creative.

DATE : ___ / ___ / _____

3 WINS FROM YESTERDAY

1. ________________________________

2. ________________________________

3. ________________________________

20%

80%

3 PRIORITIES FOR TODAY

PRIORITY #1

Outcome ______________________ Time

Action ______________________ Achieved

PRIORITY #2

Outcome ______________________ Time

Action ______________________ Achieved

PRIORITY #3

Outcome ______________________ Time

Action ______________________ Achieved

QUESTIONS / NOTES

Stay Curious. Stay Creative.

Your Focus +

Your Self Discipline

= Your Success.

DATE : ___ / ___ / _____

3 WINS FROM YESTERDAY

1. ____

2. ____

3. ____

20%

80%

3 PRIORITIES FOR TODAY

PRIORITY #1

Outcome ______________________________ Time

Action _______________________________ Achieved

PRIORITY #2

Outcome ______________________________ Time

Action _______________________________ Achieved

PRIORITY #3

Outcome ______________________________ Time

Action _______________________________ Achieved

____

____

QUESTIONS / NOTES

Stay Curious. Stay Creative.

DATE : ___ / ___ / _____

3 WINS FROM YESTERDAY

1. ____

2. ____

3. ____

20%
80%

3 PRIORITIES FOR TODAY

PRIORITY #1

Outcome ______________________________ Time ☐

Action ______________________________ Achieved ☐

PRIORITY #2

Outcome ______________________________ Time ☐

Action ______________________________ Achieved ☐

PRIORITY #3

Outcome ______________________________ Time ☐

Action ______________________________ Achieved ☐

____

____

QUESTIONS / NOTES

Stay Curious. Stay Creative.

DATE : ___ / ___ / _____

3 WINS FROM YESTERDAY

1. ______________________________

2. ______________________________

3. ______________________________

20%
80%

3 PRIORITIES FOR TODAY

PRIORITY #1

Outcome ______________________ Time

Action ______________________ Achieved

PRIORITY #2

Outcome ______________________ Time

Action ______________________ Achieved

PRIORITY #3

Outcome ______________________ Time

Action ______________________ Achieved

____

____

QUESTIONS / NOTES

Stay Curious. Stay Creative.

DATE : ___ / ___ / _____

3 WINS FROM YESTERDAY

1. ______________________________

2. ______________________________

3. ______________________________

20%
80%

3 PRIORITIES FOR TODAY

PRIORITY #1

Outcome ______________________ Time ☐

Action ______________________ Achieved ☐

PRIORITY #2

Outcome ______________________ Time ☐

Action ______________________ Achieved ☐

PRIORITY #3

Outcome ______________________ Time ☐

Action ______________________ Achieved ☐

____

____

QUESTIONS / NOTES

Stay Curious. Stay Creative.

DATE : ___ / ___ / _____

3 WINS FROM YESTERDAY

1. ______________________________

2. ______________________________

3. ______________________________

20% 80%

3 PRIORITIES FOR TODAY

PRIORITY #1

Outcome ______________________ Time

Action ______________________ Achieved

PRIORITY #2

Outcome ______________________ Time

Action ______________________ Achieved

PRIORITY #3

Outcome ______________________ Time

Action ______________________ Achieved

____

____

QUESTIONS / NOTES

Stay Curious. Stay Creative.

Purge

emails

daily.

DATE : ___ / ___ / _____

3 WINS FROM YESTERDAY

1. ______________________________

2. ______________________________

3. ______________________________

20%
80%

3 PRIORITIES FOR TODAY

PRIORITY #1

Outcome ______________________ Time

Action ______________________ Achieved

PRIORITY #2

Outcome ______________________ Time

Action ______________________ Achieved

PRIORITY #3

Outcome ______________________ Time

Action ______________________ Achieved

____

____

QUESTIONS / NOTES

Stay Curious. Stay Creative.

DATE : ___ / ___ / _____

3 WINS FROM YESTERDAY

1. ____

2. ____

3. ____

20% 80%

3 PRIORITIES FOR TODAY

PRIORITY #1

Outcome ______________________________ Time

Action ______________________________ Achieved

PRIORITY #2

Outcome ______________________________ Time

Action ______________________________ Achieved

PRIORITY #3

Outcome ______________________________ Time

Action ______________________________ Achieved

____

____

QUESTIONS / NOTES

Stay Curious. Stay Creative.

DATE : ___ / ___ / _____

3 WINS FROM YESTERDAY

1. ______________________________

2. ______________________________

3. ______________________________

20%
80%

3 PRIORITIES FOR TODAY

PRIORITY #1

Outcome ______________________ Time

Action ______________________ Achieved

PRIORITY #2

Outcome ______________________ Time

Action ______________________ Achieved

PRIORITY #3

Outcome ______________________ Time

Action ______________________ Achieved

____

____

QUESTIONS / NOTES

Stay Curious. Stay Creative.

DATE : ___ / ___ / _____

3 WINS FROM YESTERDAY

1. ______________________________

2. ______________________________

3. ______________________________

3 PRIORITIES FOR TODAY

20%

80%

PRIORITY #1

Outcome ______________________ Time

Action ______________________ Achieved

PRIORITY #2

Outcome ______________________ Time

Action ______________________ Achieved

PRIORITY #3

Outcome ______________________ Time

Action ______________________ Achieved

____

____

QUESTIONS / NOTES

Stay Curious. Stay Creative.

DATE : ___ / ___ / _____

3 WINS FROM YESTERDAY

1. ______________________________________

2. ______________________________________

3. ______________________________________

20%
80%

3 PRIORITIES FOR TODAY

PRIORITY #1

Outcome ____________________________ Time

Action ______________________________ Achieved

PRIORITY #2

Outcome ____________________________ Time

Action ______________________________ Achieved

PRIORITY #3

Outcome ____________________________ Time

Action ______________________________ Achieved

QUESTIONS / NOTES

Stay Curious. Stay Creative.

Practicing

saying,

"Not right now."

DATE : ___ / ___ / _____

3 WINS FROM YESTERDAY

1. ________________________________

2. ________________________________

3. ________________________________

20%
80%

3 PRIORITIES FOR TODAY

PRIORITY #1

Outcome ________________________ Time

Action __________________________ Achieved

PRIORITY #2

Outcome ________________________ Time

Action __________________________ Achieved

PRIORITY #3

Outcome ________________________ Time

Action __________________________ Achieved

____

____

QUESTIONS / NOTES

Stay Curious. Stay Creative.

DATE : ___ / ___ / _____

3 WINS FROM YESTERDAY

1. ______________________________

2. ______________________________

3. ______________________________

3 PRIORITIES FOR TODAY

20%
80%

PRIORITY #1

Outcome ______________________ Time

Action ______________________ Achieved

PRIORITY #2

Outcome ______________________ Time

Action ______________________ Achieved

PRIORITY #3

Outcome ______________________ Time

Action ______________________ Achieved

QUESTIONS / NOTES

Stay Curious. Stay Creative.

DATE : ___ / ___ / _____

3 WINS FROM YESTERDAY

1. ______________________________

2. ______________________________

3. ______________________________

20% 80%

3 PRIORITIES FOR TODAY

PRIORITY #1

Outcome ______________________ Time

Action ______________________ Achieved

PRIORITY #2

Outcome ______________________ Time

Action ______________________ Achieved

PRIORITY #3

Outcome ______________________ Time

Action ______________________ Achieved

____

____

QUESTIONS / NOTES

Stay Curious. Stay Creative.

DATE : ___ / ___ / _____

3 WINS FROM YESTERDAY

1. ______________________________

2. ______________________________

3. ______________________________

3 PRIORITIES FOR TODAY

PRIORITY #1

Outcome ______________________ Time

Action ______________________ Achieved

PRIORITY #2

Outcome ______________________ Time

Action ______________________ Achieved

PRIORITY #3

Outcome ______________________ Time

Action ______________________ Achieved

____

____

QUESTIONS / NOTES

Stay Curious. Stay Creative.

DATE : ___ / ___ / _____

3 WINS FROM YESTERDAY

1. ______________________________

2. ______________________________

3. ______________________________

20%
80%

3 PRIORITIES FOR TODAY

PRIORITY #1

Outcome ______________________ Time

Action ______________________ Achieved

PRIORITY #2

Outcome ______________________ Time

Action ______________________ Achieved

PRIORITY #3

Outcome ______________________ Time

Action ______________________ Achieved

____

____

QUESTIONS / NOTES

Stay Curious. Stay Creative.

Preparation

begets

confidence

DATE : ___ / ___ / _____

3 WINS FROM YESTERDAY

1. ______________________________

2. ______________________________

3. ______________________________

3 PRIORITIES FOR TODAY

20%
80%

PRIORITY #1

Outcome ______________________ Time

Action ______________________ Achieved

PRIORITY #2

Outcome ______________________ Time

Action ______________________ Achieved

PRIORITY #3

Outcome ______________________ Time

Action ______________________ Achieved

QUESTIONS / NOTES

Stay Curious. Stay Creative.

DATE : ___ / ___ / _____

3 WINS FROM YESTERDAY

1. ______________________________

2. ______________________________

3. ______________________________

20% 80%

3 PRIORITIES FOR TODAY

PRIORITY #1

Outcome ______________________ Time

Action ______________________ Achieved

PRIORITY #2

Outcome ______________________ Time

Action ______________________ Achieved

PRIORITY #3

Outcome ______________________ Time

Action ______________________ Achieved

____

____

QUESTIONS / NOTES

Stay Curious. Stay Creative.

DATE : ___ / ___ / _____

3 WINS FROM YESTERDAY

1. ____

2. ____

3. ____

20% 80%

3 PRIORITIES FOR TODAY

PRIORITY #1

Outcome ______________________________ Time

Action ______________________________ Achieved

PRIORITY #2

Outcome ______________________________ Time

Action ______________________________ Achieved

PRIORITY #3

Outcome ______________________________ Time

Action ______________________________ Achieved

____

____

QUESTIONS / NOTES

Stay Curious. Stay Creative.

DATE : ___ / ___ / _____

3 WINS FROM YESTERDAY

1. ____

2. ____

3. ____

20%
80%

3 PRIORITIES FOR TODAY

PRIORITY #1

Outcome ______________________________ Time

Action ______________________________ Achieved

PRIORITY #2

Outcome ______________________________ Time

Action ______________________________ Achieved

PRIORITY #3

Outcome ______________________________ Time

Action ______________________________ Achieved

____

____

QUESTIONS / NOTES

Stay Curious. Stay Creative.

DATE : ___ / ___ / _____

3 WINS FROM YESTERDAY

1. ______________________________

2. ______________________________

3. ______________________________

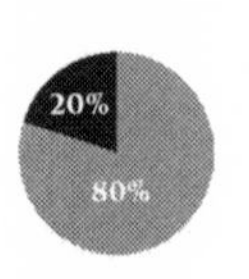

3 PRIORITIES FOR TODAY

PRIORITY #1

Outcome ______________________ Time [ ]

Action ______________________ Achieved [ ]

PRIORITY #2

Outcome ______________________ Time [ ]

Action ______________________ Achieved [ ]

PRIORITY #3

Outcome ______________________ Time [ ]

Action ______________________ Achieved [ ]

____

____

QUESTIONS / NOTES

Stay Curious. Stay Creative.

The key in the
80/20 rule

is knowing what
activities give you the

***most significant
impact and
value.***

Date : ___ / ___ / _____

3 Wins From Yesterday

1. ______________________________________

2. ______________________________________

3. ______________________________________

20%
80%

3 PRIORITIES FOR TODAY

Priority #1

Outcome ____________________________ Time

Action ______________________________ Achieved

Priority #2

Outcome ____________________________ Time

Action ______________________________ Achieved

Priority #3

Outcome ____________________________ Time

Action ______________________________ Achieved

____

____

QUESTIONS / NOTES

Stay Curious. Stay Creative.

Date : ___ / ___ / _____

3 Wins From Yesterday

1. ________________________________

2. ________________________________

3. ________________________________

20%

80%

3 PRIORITIES FOR TODAY

Priority #1

Outcome ________________________ Time

Action ________________________ Achieved

Priority #2

Outcome ________________________ Time

Action ________________________ Achieved

Priority #3

Outcome ________________________ Time

Action ________________________ Achieved

QUESTIONS / NOTES

Stay Curious. Stay Creative.

DATE : ___ / ___ / _____

3 WINS FROM YESTERDAY

1. ______________________________

2. ______________________________

3. ______________________________

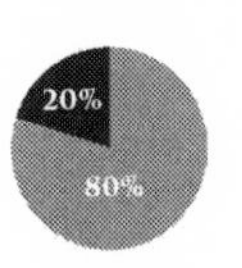

3 PRIORITIES FOR TODAY

PRIORITY #1

Outcome ______________________ Time [ ]

Action ______________________ Achieved [ ]

PRIORITY #2

Outcome ______________________ Time [ ]

Action ______________________ Achieved [ ]

PRIORITY #3

Outcome ______________________ Time [ ]

Action ______________________ Achieved [ ]

____

____

QUESTIONS / NOTES

Stay Curious. Stay Creative.

DATE : ___ / ___ / _____

3 WINS FROM YESTERDAY

1. ______________________________
2. ______________________________
3. ______________________________

20%
80%

3 PRIORITIES FOR TODAY

PRIORITY #1

Outcome ______________________ Time

Action ______________________ Achieved

PRIORITY #2

Outcome ______________________ Time

Action ______________________ Achieved

PRIORITY #3

Outcome ______________________ Time

Action ______________________ Achieved

____

____

QUESTIONS / NOTES

Stay Curious. Stay Creative.

DATE : ___ / ___ / _____

3 WINS FROM YESTERDAY

1. ______________________________

2. ______________________________

3. ______________________________

20%
80%

3 PRIORITIES FOR TODAY

PRIORITY #1

Outcome ______________________ Time

Action ______________________ Achieved

PRIORITY #2

Outcome ______________________ Time

Action ______________________ Achieved

PRIORITY #3

Outcome ______________________ Time

Action ______________________ Achieved

QUESTIONS / NOTES

Stay Curious. Stay Creative.

The less
frequently

you check your email,

***the more
productive day***

you'll have.

DATE : ___ / ___ / _____

3 WINS FROM YESTERDAY

1. ______________________________

2. ______________________________

3. ______________________________

3 PRIORITIES FOR TODAY

PRIORITY #1

Outcome ______________________ Time

Action ______________________ Achieved

PRIORITY #2

Outcome ______________________ Time

Action ______________________ Achieved

PRIORITY #3

Outcome ______________________ Time

Action ______________________ Achieved

QUESTIONS / NOTES

Stay Curious. Stay Creative.

DATE : ___ / ___ / _____

3 WINS FROM YESTERDAY

1. ______________________________

2. ______________________________

3. ______________________________

20% 80%

3 PRIORITIES FOR TODAY

PRIORITY #1

Outcome ______________________ Time

Action ______________________ Achieved

PRIORITY #2

Outcome ______________________ Time

Action ______________________ Achieved

PRIORITY #3

Outcome ______________________ Time

Action ______________________ Achieved

____

____

QUESTIONS / NOTES

Stay Curious. Stay Creative.

DATE : ___ / ___ / _____

3 WINS FROM YESTERDAY

1. ______________________________

2. ______________________________

3. ______________________________

3 PRIORITIES FOR TODAY

20%
80%

PRIORITY #1

Outcome ______________________ Time

Action ______________________ Achieved

PRIORITY #2

Outcome ______________________ Time

Action ______________________ Achieved

PRIORITY #3

Outcome ______________________ Time

Action ______________________ Achieved

____

____

QUESTIONS / NOTES

Stay Curious. Stay Creative.

DATE : ___ / ___ / _____

3 WINS FROM YESTERDAY

1. ______________________________

2. ______________________________

3. ______________________________

3 PRIORITIES FOR TODAY

20%

80%

PRIORITY #1

Outcome ______________________ Time

Action ______________________ Achieved

PRIORITY #2

Outcome ______________________ Time

Action ______________________ Achieved

PRIORITY #3

Outcome ______________________ Time

Action ______________________ Achieved

____

____

QUESTIONS / NOTES

Stay Curious. Stay Creative.

DATE : ___ / ___ / _____

3 WINS FROM YESTERDAY

1. ______________________________

2. ______________________________

3. ______________________________

3 PRIORITIES FOR TODAY

20%
80%

PRIORITY #1

Outcome ______________________ Time

Action ______________________ Achieved

PRIORITY #2

Outcome ______________________ Time

Action ______________________ Achieved

PRIORITY #3

Outcome ______________________ Time

Action ______________________ Achieved

____

____

QUESTIONS / NOTES

Stay Curious. Stay Creative.

Made in the USA
Columbia, SC
29 January 2020

87241398R00093